PROSLOGION

Anselm

Copyright © 2014 Beloved Publishing

All rights reserved. No part of this book may be reproduced, scanned, or distributed in any printed or electronic form without permission.

Printed in the United States of America

ISBN:1631740393

Preface

I formerly published, at the instance of certain of my brethren, a little work, in which, assuming the person of one who by silent reasoning with himself is searching for a knowledge he does not yet possess, I gave an example of the manner in which we may meditate concerning the grounds of our faith. But afterwards, when I considered that this work was put together by the interweaving of a great number of arguments, I began to ask myself whether there might not perhaps be found some one argument which should have no need of any other argument beside itself to prove it, and might suffice by itself to demonstrate that God really exists and is the Supreme Good, which needeth nothing beside itself to give it being or well-being, but without which nothing else can have either the one or the other; and whereof all other things are true which we believe concerning the divine essence. And when after many times earnestly directing my thoughts to this matter, it sometimes seemed to me that what I sought was just within my grasp, but sometimes that it eluded my mind's sight altogether, at last I resolved in despair to renounce the search for a thing, the discovery whereof was beyond my powers. But this train of thought, so soon as I desired to lay it aside lest it should hinder my mind while vainly occupied therein from attending to other matters which might be more profitable to me, at once began to press itself as it were importunately upon me, unwilling and reluctant as I was to entertain it. And so one day, when I was wearied out with violently resisting this importunity, in the midst of the struggle of my thoughts, there so presented itself to me the very thing which I had given up hope of finding, that I hastened to embrace that very train of thought which I was but a moment ago anxiously thrusting from me. Thinking therefore that if I wrote down what I so greatly rejoiced to have found, it would please others who might read it, I wrote the following little work, treating of this and of some other matters, in the character of one striving to raise his thoughts to the contemplation of God and seeking to understand what he already believes. And because neither this nor the other treatise which I mentioned before, seemed to me worthy to be called a book or to have the writer's name set in the front of it, and yet I thought I must not let them go without some title to invite those to read into whose hands they might come, I gave a name to each, calling the former An example of meditation on the grounds of faith and the latter Faith in search of Understanding. But, when both had been often transcribed under these titles by divers persons, was constrained by many and especially by Hugh the reverend Archbishop of Lyons and Legate of the Apostolic See in Gaul, who laid his commands upon me in virtue of his apostolical authority, to prefix my name to them. And so that this might be done more fittingly, I have called the former Monologion, that is, The Soliloquy, and this Proslogion, that is, The Address.

Chapter I

Come now, thou poor child of man, turn awhile from thy business, hide thyself for a little time from restless thoughts, cast away thy troublesome cares, put aside thy wearisome distractions. Give thyself a little leisure to converse with God, and take thy rest awhile in Him. Enter into the secret chamber of thy heart: leave everything without but God and what may help thee to seek after Him, and when thou hast shut the door, then do thou seek Him. Say now, O my whole heart, say now to God, I seek Thy face; Thy face, Lord, do I seek. Come now then, O Lord my God, teach Thou my heart when and how I may seek Thee, where and how I may find Thee? O Lord, if Thou art not here, where else shall I seek Thee? but if Thou art everywhere, why do I not behold Thee, since Thou art here present? Surely indeed Thou dwellest in the light which no man can approach unto. But where is that light unapproachable? or how may I approach unto it since it is unapproachable? or who shall lead me and bring me into it that I may see Thee therein? Again, by what tokens shall I know Thee, in what form shall I look for Thee? I have never seen Thee, O Lord my God; I know not Thy form. What shall I do then, O Lord most high, what shall I do, banished as I am so far from Thee? What shall Thy servant do that is sick for love of Thee, and yet is cast away from Thy presence? He panteth to behold Thee, and yet Thy presence is very far from him. He longeth to approach unto Thee, and yet Thy dwelling-place is unapproachable. He desireth to find Thee, yet he knoweth not Thy habitation. He would fain seek Thee, yet he knoweth not Thy face. O Lord, Thou art my God, Thou art my Lord; and I have never beheld Thee. Thou hast created me and created me anew, and all good things that I have, hast Thou bestowed upon me, and yet I have never known Thee. Nay, I was created to behold Thee, and yet have I never unto this day done that for the sake whereof I was created. O miserable lot of man, to have lost that whereunto he was created! O hard and terrible condition! Alas, what hath he lost? what hath he found? what hath departed from him? what hath continued with him? He hath lost the blessedness whereunto he was created, and he hath found the misery whereunto he was not created; that without which nothing is happy, hath departed from him, and that hath continued with him which by itself cannot but be miserable. Once man did eat angels' food, after which he now hungereth; now he eateth the bread of affliction, which then he knew not. Alas for the common woe of man, the universal sorrow of the children of Adam! Our first father was filled with abundance, we sigh with hunger; he was rich, we are beggars. He miserably threw away that in the possession whereof he was happy, and in the lack whereof we are miserable; after which we lamentably long and alas! abide unsatisfied. Why did he not keep for us, when he might easily have kept it that the loss whereof so grievously afflicts us? Wherefore did he so overcloud our day, and plunge us into darkness? Why did he take from us our life, and bring upon us the pains of death? Wretches that we are, whence have we been driven out and whither? From our native country into banishment, from the vision of God into blindness, from the joy of immortality into the bitterness and horror of death. How sad the change from so great good to so great evil! Grievous is the loss, grievous the pain, grievous every thing. But alas for me, one of the miserable children of Eve, cast far away from God! What did I begin? and what have I accomplished? At what did I aim? and unto what have I attained? To what did I aspire? and where am I now sighing? I sought good, and behold, trouble I aimed at God, and have stumbled upon myself. I sought rest in my secret chamber, and I have found tribulation and grief in the inmost parts. I desired to laugh for gladness of spirit and am constrained to roar for the disquietness of my heart. I hoped for joy and behold increase of sorrow. How long, O Lord, how long? How long, O Lord, wilt Thou forget us, how long wilt Thou hide Thy face from us? When wilt Thou turn and hearken unto us? When wilt thou enlighten our eyes and show us Thy face? When wilt Thou restore Thy presence to us? Turn and took upon us, O Lord: hearken unto us, enlighten us, show us Thyself. Restore to us Thy presence that it may be well with us; for without Thee it goeth very ill with us. Have pity upon our labours and strivings after Thee, for without Thee we can do nothing. Thou callest us; help us to obey the call. I beseech Thee, O Lord, that I may not despair in my sighing, but may draw full breath again in hope. My heart is embittered by its desolation; with Thy consolation, I beseech Thee, O Lord, make it sweet again. I beseech Thee, O Lord, for in my hunger I have begun to seek Thee, suffer me not to depart from Thee fasting. I have come to Thee fainting for lack of food; let me not go empty away. I have come to Thee, as the poor man to the rich, as the miserable to the merciful, let me not return unsatisfied and despised: and if before I be fed, I sigh, grant me that, though after I have sighed, I may be fed. O Lord, I am bent downwards, I cannot look up: raise me up, that I may lift mine eyes to heaven. My iniquities are gone over my head, they overwhelm me; they are like a sore burden too heavy for me to bear. Deliver me, take away my burden, lest the pit of my wickedness shut its mouth upon me: grant unto me that I may look upon Thy light, though from afar off, though out of the deep. I will seek Thee, with longing after Thee. I will long after Thee in seeking Thee, I will find Thee by loving Thee, I will love Thee in finding Thee. I confess to Thee, O Lord, and I give thanks unto Thee, because Thou hast created in me this Thine image, that I may remember Thee, think upon Thee, love Thee: but so darkened is Thine image in me by the smoke of my sins that it cannot do that whereunto it was created, unless Thou renew it and create it again. I seek not, O Lord, to search out Thy depth, but I desire in some measure to understand Thy truth, which my heart believeth and loveth. Nor do I seek to understand that I may believe, but I believe that I may understand. For this too I believe, that unless I first believe, I shall not understand.

Chapter II

Therefore, O Lord, who grantest to faith understanding, grant unto me that, so far as Thou knowest it to be expedient for me, I may understand that Thou art, as we believe; and also that Thou art what we believe Thee to be. And of a truth we believe that Thou art somewhat than which no greater can be conceived. Is there then nothing real that can be thus described? for the fool hath said in his heart, There is no God. Yet surely even that fool himself when he hears me speak of somewhat than which nothing greater can be conceived under stands what he hears, and what he understands is in his understanding, even if he do not under stand that it really exists. It is one thing for a thing to be in the understanding, and another to understand that the thing really exists. For when a painter considers the work which he is to make, he has it indeed in his understanding; but he doth not yet understand that really to exist which as yet he has not made. But when he has painted his picture, then he both has the picture in his understanding, and also under stands it really to exist. Thus even the fool is certain that something exists, at least in his understanding, than which nothing greater can be conceived; because, when he hears this mentioned, he understands it, and whatsoever is understood, exists in the understanding. And surely that than which no greater can be conceived cannot exist only in the understanding. For if it exist indeed in the understanding only, it can be thought to exist also in reality; and real existence is more than existence in the under standing only. If then that than which no greater can be conceived exists in the understanding only, then that than which no greater can be conceived is something a greater than which can be conceived: but this is impossible. There fore it is certain that something than which no greater can be conceived exists both in the under standing and also in reality.

Chapter III

Not only does this something than which no greater can be conceived exist, but it exists in so true a sense that it cannot even be conceived not to exist. For it is possible to form the conception of an object whose non-existence shall be inconceivable; and such an object is of necessity greater than any object whose existence is conceivable: wherefore if that than which no greater can be conceived can be conceived not to exist; it follows that that than which no greater can be conceived is not that than which no greater can be conceived [for there can be thought a greater than it, namely, an object whose non-existence shall be inconceivable]; and this brings us to a contradiction. And thus it is proved that that thing than which no greater can be conceived exists in so true a sense, that it cannot even be conceived not to exist: and this thing art Thou, O Lord our God! And so Thou, O Lord my God, existest in so true a sense that Thou canst not even be conceived not to exist. And this is as is fitting. For if any mind could conceive aught better than Thee, then the creature would be ascending above the Creator, and judging the Creator; which is a supposition very absurd. Thou therefore dost exist in a truer sense than all else beside Thee, and art more real than all else beside Thee; because whatsoever else existeth, existeth in a less true sense than Thou, and therefore is less real than Thou. Why then said the fool in his heart, There is no God, when it is so plain to a rational mind that Thou art more real than any thing else? Why, except that he is a fool indeed?

Chapter IV

But how came the fool to say in his heart that which he could not conceive? or how came he to be able not to conceive that which yet he said in his heart? For it may be thought that to conceive and to say in one's heart are one and the same thing. If it is true—nay, because it is true, that he conceived it, because he said it in his heart; and also true that he did not say it in his heart because he could not conceive it; it follows that there are two senses in which something may be understood to be conceived or said in the heart. For in one sense we are said to have a conception of something, when we have a conception of the word that signifies it; and in another sense, when we understand what the thing really is. In the former sense then we may say that God is conceived not to exist: but in the latter, He cannot by any means be conceived not to exist. For no man that understandeth what fire and water mean, can conceive that fire is really water; though he may have this conception, as far as the words go. Thus in like manner no man that understandeth what God is can conceive that God does not exist; although he may say these words [that God does not exist] either with no meaning at all, or with some other meaning than that which they properly bear. For God is that than which no greater can be conceived. He who well under standeth what this is, certainly understandeth it to be such as cannot even be conceived not to exist. Whosoever therefore understandeth in this way that God exists, cannot conceive that he does not exist. Thanks be to Thee, O good Lord, thanks be to Thee! because that which heretofore I believed by Thy grace, I now by Thine illumination thus understand, so that, even though I should not wish to believe in Thine existence, I cannot but understand that Thou dost exist.

Chapter V

What then art Thou Lord God, Thou than which nothing greater can be conceived? What indeed but that Supreme Good which being alone of all things self-existent, didst make all other things beside Thee out of nothing? For whatsoever is not this is less than can be conceived: but Thou canst not be conceived to be less than the highest conceivable. What good thing is lacking to the Supreme Good, whereon depends the being of every good thing beside? Thou therefore art righteous, true, blessed, and hast all attributes which it is better to have than to be without; for it is better to be righteous than not righteous, and blessed than not blessed.

Chapter VI

But since it is better to have perception or to have omnipotence, to be pitiful or to be without passions, than not to have these attributes; how hast Thou perception, if Thou art not a body? or omnipotence, if Thou canst not do everything? or how art Thou at one and the same time pitiful and without passions? For if only bodily things have perception, since the senses with which we perceive belong and attach to the body; how canst Thou have perception, since Thou art not a body but the Supreme Spirit, which is higher than a body can be? But if perception is only knowledge or a means towards knowledge; since he who perceives, has knowledge thereby, according to the special character of the senses, by sight of colours, by taste of savours and so forth: then whatsoever has knowledge in whatsoever manner may be said without impropriety in some sense to perceive. Therefore, O Lord, although Thou art not a body, yet of a truth Thou hast in this sense perception in the highest degree, since Thou knowest all things in the highest degree; but not in the sense wherein an animal that has knowledge by means of bodily feeling is said to have perception.

Chapter VII

But again, how canst Thou be omnipotent, if Thou canst not do all things? Yet if Thou canst not suffer corruption, canst not lie, canst not make what is true to be false, or what is done, undone, and so forth; how canst Thou do all things? Or shall we say that to be capable of these would be not power but rather impotence? For he who can do these, can do what is not expedient for him, and what he ought not; and the more he can do what is not expedient for him and what he ought not, the more power have evil and wickedness over him, and the less power hath he against them. He therefore that can do such things, can do them in virtue not of power but of impotence. For he is said to be able to do them, not because he himself has power in doing them, but because his impotence gives something else power to work in him; or else in an improper way of speaking, such as we often use when we put to be for not to be, and to do for not to do or to do nothing. For we often say to one who says that a thing is not such-and-such: It is as you say it is; when it would seem more proper to say, It is not as you say it is not. Again we say: This man sits, as that man does; or This man rests as that man does: though sitting is a kind of not doing, and resting is doing nothing. Thus then when a man is said to have the power of doing or undergoing what is not expedient for him or what he ought not, the word power signifies impotence; since the more power of this sort he hath, the more power have evil and wickedness against him, and the less hath he against them.

Therefore, O Lord God, Thou art all the more truly omnipotent, that Thou canst do nothing that is done through impotence, and nothing hath any power against Thee.

Chapter VIII

Once again, how art Thou at the same time pitiful and yet without passions? For unless Thou have passions, Thou wilt not have compassion; if Thou hast not compassion, Thy heart is not made sorry by compassion, that is by fellow-feeling with the sorrowful; and this is what pity is. Yet if Thou art not pitiful, whence have the sorrowful so great consolation from Thee? How then canst Thou at once be and not be pitiful, O Lord, unless because Thou art pitiful in respect of us, and art not pitiful in respect of Thyself? For Thou art pitiful to our apprehension, and art not pitiful to Thine own. For when Thou hast respect to us in our sorrow, we perceive the effects of pity; but Thou feelest not the emotion thereof. And thus Thou art pitiful in that Thou savest the wretched, and sparest those that sin against Thee; and yet again Thou art not moved by a fellow-feeling with our misery.

Chapter IX

Again, how dost Thou spare the wicked, if Thou art wholly and supremely just? For how dost Thou, being wholly and supremely just, do aught that is not just? And what manner of justice is that, to give eternal life to one that deserves eternal death? Whence then, O good God, good both to the good and to the evil, whence is it that Thou savest the evil, if to save the evil is not just, and yet Thou doest nothing that is not just? Or is it because Thy goodness is incomprehensible that this lieth hid in that light unapproachable which is Thy dwelling-place? Verily it is in the most deep and secret abyss of Thy goodness that there lieth hid the fountain, whence floweth the river of Thy mercy. For though Thou art wholly and supremely just, yet art Thou also gracious to the wicked, because Thou art wholly and supremely good. For Thou wouldest be less good, if Thou wert not gracious to any that was evil.

For better is he who is good both to the good and to the evil than he who is good to the good only; and better is he who is good to the evil both in punishing and in sparing them, than he who is good in punishing them only. There fore Thou art pitiful because Thou art wholly and supremely good. And although perchance we suppose that we see reason why Thou dost reward good to the good and evil to the evil, yet certainly we must be filled with wonder why Thou, being wholly and supremely just and having need of nothing, renderest good to the evil and those who have sinned against Thee. O the depth of Thy goodness, O God! We both see whence Thou art merciful and yet see it only in part. We perceive whence the river flows, yet behold not the fountain from which it springs. For it is of the plenitude of Thy goodness, that Thou art kind to them that have sinned against Thee; and yet it lieth hid in the depth of Thy goodness wherefore this is so. Verily although it is in Thy goodness that Thou rewardest good to the good, and evil to the evil; yet this the rule of justice seems to require. But when

Thou rewardest good to the evil, then we know that the supremely Good willed to do that, yet wonder that the supremely Just was able so to will. O thou mercy of God, from how abundant a sweetness, from how sweet an abundance flowest thou forth unto us! O boundless goodness of God, how ought we sinners to be moved by love of Thee! For Thou savest the just, justice assenting; but deliverest the wicked, when justice condemns them; Thou savest the just by the help of their deserts; Thou deliverest the wicked against their deserts; Thou savest the just, acknowledging in them the good which Thou didst give them; Thou deliverest the wicked, pardoning the evil which Thou hatest. O immeasurable goodness, passing all understanding, goodness! Let there flow into me that mercy which floweth out of that goodness. Spare in Thy mercy, and take not vengeance in Thy justice. For although it be hard to understand how Thy mercy is not parted from Thy justice; yet is it necessary to believe that it is not at enmity with Thy justice, that it floweth from Thy goodness, that it is not without justice, nay in truth accordeth with Thy justice. For if Thou art merciful only because Thou art supremely good, and art supremely good only because Thou art supremely just: therefore art Thou in truth merciful because Thou art supremely just. Help me, O just and merciful God, for I seek Thy light. Help me, that I may understand what I say! Verily then Thou art merciful because Thou art just. Is then Thy mercy born of Thy justice? Dost Thou then out of justice spare the wicked? If it be so, O Lord, if it be so, teach me how it is so. Is it because it is just that Thou shouldest so be good that Thou couldst not be conceived better, and shouldest work so mightily that Thou couldst not be conceived mightier? For what is juster than this? Yet this would not be, if Thou wert good in punishing only, not in sparing; and if Thou madest them good only that were merely not good, and not also those that were evil. And so it is just that Thou shouldst spare the wicked, and make them that were wicked to be good. Lastly, what is not done justly, ought not to be done; and what ought not to be done, is done unjustly. If then

Thou dost not have mercy on the wicked justly, then Thou hast mercy on them unjustly: and since it were blasphemy to say this, it is fit to believe that Thou hast mercy on the wicked justly.

Chapter X

But it is also just that Thou shouldest punish the wicked; for what is more just than that the good should receive good things and the evil evil things? How then is it just for Thee both to punish the wicked and also to spare them? For when Thou dost punish the wicked, it is just, because it is agreeable to their deserts; but when Thou sparest them, it is just also, because though it befitteth not their deserts, yet it befitteth Thy goodness. For in sparing the wicked Thou are just in respect of Thyself, though not in respect of us; just as Thou art pitiful in respect of us and not in respect of Thyself; since in saving us, whom Thou mightest justly destroy, Thou art pitiful; not that Thou art Thyself moved by the feeling of pity, but that we feel the effect of pity; and in the same manner Thou art just, not that Thou hast rendered to us what we have deserved, but that Thou dost what becometh Thee, the supremely Good. Thus dost Thou without contradiction punish justly and justly spare.

Chapter XI

But is it not also just even in respect of Thyself, O Lord, to punish the wicked? For it is just that Thou shouldest be so just as no man could conceive Thee juster; and this Thou wouldest by no means be, if Thou didst only render good to the good and not evil to the evil. Far juster is he that rewards the good and evil alike according to their deservings and not the good only. And so Thou art just in respect of Thyself, O just and gracious God, both when Thou punishest and when Thou sparest. Verily then all the paths of the Lord are mercy and truthand yet the Lord is just or righteous in all His ways and that without contradiction, since those whom Thou dost will to punish, it is not just should be saved: and whom Thou dost will to spare, it is not just should be condemned. For that alone is just, which Thou dost will, and that not just, which Thou wiliest not. Thus then is Thy mercy born of Thy justice, because it is just that Thou shouldest be so good as to be good even in sparing; and this is perchance why the supremely just can will good to the evil. But if it can at all be apprehended why Thou canst will to save the wicked; certainly that can by no means be comprehended why among those alike wicked Thou savest these rather than those by Thy supreme goodness and condemnest those rather than these by Thy supreme justice. Thus then hast Thou indeed perception and omnipotence, art pitiful and yet without passion; as Thou hast life, wisdom, goodness, blessedness, eternity and whatsoever other attributes it is better to have than not to have.

Chapter XII

But certainly whatsoever Thou art, this Thou art by reason of nothing else outside of Thyself. Thou therefore art the life where by Thou livest; and that wisdom whereby Thou art wise; and that very goodness, whereby Thou art good both to the good and also to the evil; and so with the rest of Thine attributes.

Chapter XIII

But everything which is anyhow comprehended in place or time, is less than that which no law of place or time restraineth. Since then there is nothing greater than Thou, no place or time comprehendeth Thee, but Thou art everywhere and always: and of Thee alone can it be said Thou alone art uncircumscribed and eternal. How then are other spirits called uncircumscribed and eternal? Thou indeed art alone eternal; because Thou alone of all beings neither beginnest nor ceasest to be. But how art Thou alone uncircumscribed? May we say that the created spirit in comparison of Thee is circumscribed, though in comparison of the body, uncircumscribed? For the body is al together circumscribed, since it is altogether in some certain place, and cannot be at the same time in any other; and this we see only in what is of the nature of body. That again is uncircumscribed, which is altogether in all places at the same time; and this is conceived to be true of Thee only. But that is at once circumscribed and uncircumscribed which being wholly in some certain place, can be at the same time wholly elsewhere; and this we know to be true of created spirits. For if the soul were not wholly in every member of its body, it would not be able wholly to have feeling in every member. Thou then, O Lord, art in a sense wherein it is true of nothing else, at once uncircumscribed and eternal; and yet other spirits also are uncircumscribed and eternal.

Chapter XIV

Hast thou then found, O my soul, that which thou wast seeking? Thou wast seeking God and thou hast found that He is that thing which is supreme among all things, than which nothing better can be conceived, and that this is very life, light, wisdom, goodness, eternal bliss and blissful eternity, and that this is everywhere and always. For if thou hast not found thy God, how can He be this which thou hast found, and which thou hast with so certain an assurance, so assured a certainty understood Him to be? But if thou hast found Him, why dost thou not perceive that which thou hast found? Why doth my soul not perceive Thee, O Lord God, if she hath found Thee? Hath she not found Thee, whom she hath found to be light and truth? Or could she understand anything at all concerning Thee, except by Thy light and truth? If then she hath seen light and truth, she hath seen Thee; if she hath not seen Thee, she hath seen neither light nor truth. Or is it rather that that which she hath seen is indeed both truth and light; and yet she hath not yet seen Thee because she hath seen Thee in part only, but hath not seen Thee as Thou art? O Lord my God, my Creator and Renewer, tell my soul that longeth after Thee, what else Thou art beside what she hath seen, that she may see clearly that after which she longeth. She stretcheth out herself that she may see more, and yet seeth nothing beyond what she hath seen, except mere darkness. Nay, she seeth not darkness, for in Thee is no darkness; but she seeth that she can see no farther, because of the darkness which is in herself.

Wherefore is this, O Lord, wherefore is this? Are her eyes darkened by her own infirmity, or are they dazzled by Thy splendour? Surely she is both darkened in herself and dazzled by Thee. Thus also she is darkened by reason of her own littleness, and overwhelmed by reason of Thine immeasurable greatness. She is straitened by her own narrowness, and vanquished by Thy vastness. For how great is that Light, whereby every truth shineth that doth enlighten the rational intelligence! How vast is that Truth, wherein is contained every thing that is true, and outside whereof is only nothingness and falsehood! How immeasurable is that Vision which beholdeth in one glance all things that have been created and whence and by whom and how they were created out of nothing! What purity, what simplicity, what clearness and splendour is there! Surely more than can be comprehended by any creature.

Chapter XV

Therefore, O Lord, not only art Thou that than which no greater can be conceived, but Thou art something greater than can be conceived. For because there may be conceived to be something greater than can be conceived; if Thou art not that something, there may be conceived something greater than Thee; which is impossible.

Chapter XVI

Verily, O Lord, this is the light unapproachable, wherein Thou dwellest; for of a truth there is nothing beside Thyself that can enter into that light, there to behold Thee in Thy fulness. Verily then I see not that light, for it is too great for me; and yet what soever I see, I see by means of that light; even as a weak eye seeth what it doth see by means of the sun's light, yet cannot look upon that light as it is in the sun himself. My under standing cannot attain to that light unapproachable; it is too bright for it, it taketh it not in, nor can my soul's eye bear long to be directed toward it. It is dazzled by the brightness, vanquished by the vastness, overwhelmed by the immensity, confounded by the compass thereof.

O supreme and unapproachable Light! O entire and blessed Truth! how far off art Thou from me, who am so near to Thee! How far removed art Thou from my sight, who am wholly present to Thine? Thou art everywhere wholly present, yet I see Thee not. In Thee I move, in Thee I have my being; yet can I not approach unto Thee. Thou art within me and about me, yet I perceive Thee not.

Chapter XVII

Hitherto, O Lord, Thou art hid from my soul in Thine own light and bliss; and therefore she goeth up and down in her darkness and misery. For she looketh about her, and beholdeth not Thy beauty. She listeneth, and heareth not Thy harmony. She smelleth and perceiveth not Thy sweetness. She tasteth, and hath no sense of Thy goodness. She toucheth, and feeleth not Thy smoothness. For Thou hast all these, beauty to the sight, harmony to the ear, sweetness to the smell, goodness to the taste, smoothness to the touch, all in Thee, O Lord God, in Thine own ineffable way, since it is Thou who hast granted to sensible things to have them in their own way which our bodily senses perceive; but the senses of my soul are stiffened and dulled and obstructed by the long sickness of sin.

Chapter XVIII

And once more behold, trouble! So once more cometh sorrow and grief to me that sought after joy and gladness. My soul hoped but now to be filled, and behold, once more is she bowed down by want. I sought to eat and be satisfied, and lo, I am more hungry than before. I strove to rise up into the light of God, and have fallen back into mine own darkness. Nay, not only have I fallen into the darkness, but I perceive myself encompassed about thereby. I fell into it before my mother conceived me. Surely I was conceived in darkness, and was born under the shadow there of. Surely we all fell in him, in whom we all have sinned. We all lost in him who might easily have kept it and lost it to his own sorrow and ours, that which when we desire to seek, we know not: when we seek, we find not: when we find, is not that which we seek. Help me then, according to Thy goodness! Lord, I have sought Thy face; Thy face, Lord, will I seek; O hide not Thou Thy face from me. Raise me up out of myself unto Thee. Cleanse, heal, quicken, enlighten the eye of my mind that it may look upon Thee. Grant that my soul may collect her strength once more and with all the power of her understanding strive after Thee, O Lord. What art Thou, O Lord, what art Thou? How shall my heart understand what Thou art? Surely Thou art life and wisdom and truth and goodness and blessedness and eternity and everything that is truly good. These indeed are many; but my narrow understanding cannot see so many good things in one apprehension at one and the same time, so as to be delighted by the presence of all at once. How then, O Lord, art Thou all these? Are they parts of Thee, or is rather everyone of these wholly what Thou art? For whatsoever is composed of parts is not in all respects one, but in a certain respect many and diverse from itself; and either actually or in thought can be dissolved: but to be many and not one, or to be capable of dissolution even in thought is far from Thy nature, since Thou art that than which no better can be conceived. Thus there are no parts in Thee, O Lord, nor art Thou many and not one: but Thou art one and the same with Thyself, so that in nothing art Thou unlike Thyself, nay, rather Thou art very Oneness, indivisible by any understanding. Therefore life and wisdom and Thine other attributes are not parts of Thee but are all one, and everyone of them is wholly what Thou art and what the other attributes are. And as Thou hast no parts, so neither is Thine eternity which is Thyself, at any place or time a part of Thee or of Thy whole eternity; but Thou art wholly every where and Thine eternity is wholly at all times.

Chapter XIX

But if Thou wast and art and shalt be by reason of Thine eternity; and past being is other than present being, and present being than past or future being:

how can Thine eternity be said to be wholly at all times? Or shall we say that nothing has passed away from Thine eternity so as now not to be, though once it was; nor anything to come, as though it were not as yet? Thou then wert not yesterday nor shalt be to-morrow; but yesterday and to-day and to-morrow Thou art. Nay, not even art Thou yesterday and to-day and to morrow; but Thou art, without any qualification, apart from all time; for yesterday, to-day and to-morrow are distinctions in time; but Thou, although nothing is without Thee, art nevertheless Thyself neither in place nor in time, but all things are in Thee; nothing comprehendeth Thee but Thou comprehendest all things.

Chapter XX

Thou therefore dost fill and embrace all things; Thou art before and beyond all things. And indeed Thou art before all things; because before they were made, Thou art. But how art Thou before all things? For in what manner art Thou beyond those things which are to have no end? Is it because they can in no wise be without Thee; but Thou, even though they should return into nothingness, no less art? In this way then Thou art in a manner of speaking beyond them. Or is it again because they can be conceived of as having an end, but Thou canst not? For in this way indeed they have in some sense an end; but Thou in no sense. And certainly that which in no sense hath an end is beyond that which in any sense hath an end. Dost Thou then thus also transcend all things, even though they be eternal, in that Thine eternity and theirs is present to Thee in their entirety, while they have not yet that part of their eternity which is to come, as they have no longer that part which is past. Thus Thou ever transcendest them; both in that Thou art always present to them, and because that is ever present to Thee whereunto they have not yet come is ever present with thee.

Chapter XXI

Is this what we call the age of the age or the ages of the ages? For just as the age of time comprehendeth all things that are in time, so Thine eternity comprehendeth the very ages of times themselves. And it is indeed rightly called an age, because it is one and indivisible; but also ages, because of the boundless immensity thereof. And although Thou art so great, O Lord, that all things are full of Thee and are in Thee; yet Thou art such, without being in space, so that in Thee there is neither middle nor half nor any other part.

Chapter XXII

Thou therefore alone, O Lord, art what Thou art, and who Thou art. For what is one thing in the whole and another in the parts and has in it anything subject to change, is not in all respects what it is. And whatsoever was not and begins to be, can be conceived not to be; and except something other than itself maintain it in existence, returns into nothingness; and has a past self which is not what now is; and a future self which it as yet is not; that can only be said to exist in a secondary and relative sense. But Thou art what Thou art, because whatsoever Thou art at any time or in any way, that Thou art wholly and always. And Thou art who Thou art in the primary and unqualified sense of the words; because Thou hast neither a past self nor a future self but only present self, nor canst Thou be conceived as at any time not existing. More over Thou art life and light and wisdom and blessedness and eternity and many other such like good things, and yet art but the One Supreme Good, in all respect sufficient to Thyself and needing none beside Thee, while all things beside Thee cannot without Thee have either being or well-being.

Chapter XXIII

This Good art Thou, O Thou God the Father; this Good is Thy Word, that is, Thy Son. For there can be nothing else in the Word whereby Thou utterest Thyself but what Thou art, nor anything greater or less than Thou art; because Thy Word is as true as Thou art truthful. And therefore He is as Thou art, the very Truth; not another Truth than Thyself: and Thou art so utterly without complexity in Thy nature that of Thee there cannot be born anything that is other than what Thou Thyself art. This same Good is the one mutual Love which is between Thee and Thy Son, that is, the Holy Spirit proceeding from both. For the same Love is not unequal to Thee or to Thy Son, because Thou lovest Thyself and Him, and He Himself and Thee with a Love as great as Thou art and as He is; nor can that be other than Thou and than He which is not unequal to Thyself and to Him; nor from Thy supreme simplicity of nature can there proceed anything which is other than that from which it proceedeth. But that which each Person is, that the whole Trinity, Father, Son and Holy Ghost, is at once; because each by Himself is nothing else than the supremely simple Unity and the supremely one Simplicity, which cannot be multiplied nor can be now one thing and now another. For there is one thing necessary; and doubtless this is that one thing necessary, that wherein is all good, nay rather, which is all good, the one wholly and solely Good.

Chapter XXIV

Arouse thyself, O my soul, and stir up thine understanding and consider so far as thou canst what and how great is this Good. For if particular good things are delightful, consider earnestly how delightful must be that Good which comprehendeth the pleasantness of all particular goods; and that in a pleasantness not such as we have known by experience in things created, but surpassing that no less than the Creator surpasseth the creature. For if the life that is created be good, how good must be the Life that createth! If health that is made be pleasant, how pleasant must be that Health that is the cause of all health! If the wisdom be desirable that consisteth in the knowledge of things created, how desirable must be the Wisdom that wrought all things of nothing. Lastly, if there be many great delights in things delightful, what manner of delight and how great must these be in Him who made those very things themselves that are so delightful.

Chapter XXV

O who shall enjoy this Good! And what shall he have, and what shall he lack? Surely whatsoever he wisheth he shall have and whatsoever he wisheth not, he shall be without. For there shall be goods of body and of soul, such as eye hath not seen, nor ear heard, neither have entered into the heart of man to conceive. Why then, poor child of man, dost thou wander hither and thither, seeking the goods of thy soul and body? Love the one Good wherein are all goods, and it sufficeth thee. Set thy desires upon that uncompounded Good which is all good, and it is enough. For what dost thou love, O my flesh, what dost thou desire, O my soul? If beauty delight thee, the righteous shall shine forth as the sun if swiftness or strength or freedom of body which nothing may hinder, they are as the angels of God, because it is sown a natural body, it is raised a spiritual body, spiritual, that is, in powers, not in nature. If a long life of health, there is an eternity of health; for the righteous live for evermore nd the health of the righteous cometh of the Lord. If abundance, they shall be satisfied when the glory of God shall appear.

If drunkenness, they shall be made drunken with the plenteousness of God's house. If melody, there shall the choirs of angels sing together unto God for ever and ever. If any pleasure, so it be but chaste, Thou shalt give them drink of Thy pleasures as out of the river. If wisdom, the very Wisdom of God shall manifest itself to them. If friendship, they shall love God above themselves and one an other as themselves; and God shall love them more than they love themselves; for they shall love Him and one another in Him; and He shall love Himself and them in Himself. If concord, they shall all have one will, for they shall have no will but God's will only. If power, they shall be almighty to do their own wills, even as God to do His; for as God shall be able to do what He willeth through His own power, so shall they be able to do what they will through His power; since, as they will nothing else but what He wills, so He shall will whatsoever they will; and whatsoever He willeth cannot but be. If honour and riches, God shall set His good and faithful servants over many things; yea, they shall be called sons of

God, and gods; and where His Son shall be, there also they shall be, heirs of God and joint-heirs with Christ. If true security, certainly they shall be as sure that those goods, or rather that Good, shall never and in no wise fail them as they shall be sure that they will not lose it of their own free will, and that God their lover will not take it against their wills from them that love Him, and that nothing mightier than God will separate God and them against their wills. But what manner of joy and how great a joy must there be, where there is such and so great a Good! O thou human heart, thou hungry heart, thou heart acquainted with sorrow, nay overwhelmed by sorrow, how wouldest thou rejoice if thou didst abound in all these goods! Look into thine heart and ask it whether it could contain the greatness of the joy which it would have, did it possess so great happiness. Yet surely if another whom thou didst love altogether as well as thyself, were to have the same happiness, thy joy would be doubled, since thou wouldst rejoice for him no less than for thyself. But if two or three or many more should have the same happiness, thou wouldst rejoice as much for each as for thyself, didst thou love each as thyself. There fore in that perfect mutual love of innumerable blessed angels and men, where none loveth another less than himself, each will rejoice no less for every other, than for himself. If then the heart of a man can scarce contain the joy he will have in himself in one enjoyment of so great a good, how shall it be capable of so many and so great joys? And since every man rejoiceth in the good of any in proportion as he loveth Him, as in that perfect felicity everyone will love God beyond all comparison more than he loves himself and all his fellows; so will he rejoice beyond all measure more in the felicity of God than in his own and that of all his fellows. But if they so love God with their whole heart, their whole mind, their whole soul, yet so that the whole heart, the whole mind, the whole soul shall not suffice to the excellency of the love; it will follow that they shall so rejoice with their whole heart, their whole mind, their whole soul, that their whole heart, their whole mind, their whole soul shall not suffice to the fulness of their joy.

Chapter XXVI

O my God and my Lord, my hope and the joy of my heart, tell my soul if this be the joy whereof Thou sayest unto us by Thy Son, Ask and ye shall receive, that your joy may be full. For I have found a joy that is full and more than full. For when heart and mind and soul and the whole man are full of that joy, yet shall the joy abound yet more beyond measure. Therefore that joy shall not wholly enter into them that rejoice therein; but they that rejoice shall wholly enter into that joy. Tell, O Lord, tell Thy servant inwardly in his heart, if this be the joy whereunto Thy servants shall enter, who shall enter into the joy of their Lord. But assuredly that joy, wherein Thine elect shall rejoice, eye hath not seen, nor ear heard, neither hath it entered into the heart of man. And so I have not yet uttered or conceived, O Lord, the greatness of the joy of Thy blessed ones. For their joy shall be as great as their love and their love as their knowledge. How great shall be their knowledge of Thee, O Lord, and how great their love of Thee! Surely in this life eye hath not seen, nor ear heard, neither hath it entered into the heart of man to conceive the greatness of their knowledge and love of Thee in the life to come. I pray Thee, O God, let me know Thee and love Thee so that I may rejoice in Thee. And if I cannot know Thee, love Thee, rejoice in Thee fully in this life, let me go forward from day to day, until that knowledge, love and joy at last may be full. Let the knowledge of Thee grow in me here, and there be made full; let the love of Thee increase in me here and there be full; so that my joy may here be great in hope and there full in fruition. O Lord, by Thy Son Thou dost command, nay counsel us to seek and dost promise to accept us that our joy may be full! I seek, O Lord, that which by Thy wonderful Counsellor Thou counsellest us to seek; I will accept that which Thou dost promise by Thy Truth, that my joy may be full. O Thou faithful God, I seek; grant that I may receive that my joy may be full. Meanwhile may my mind meditate thereon; may my tongue talk hereof; may my heart love it, my mouth utter it, my soul hunger after it, my flesh thirst after it, my whole substance long for it, until I enter into the joy of my Lord, three persons in one God, blessed for evermore. Amen.

Made in the USA
San Bernardino, CA
26 August 2018